# OVERCOMING
# BURNOUT

## Daily Devotionals to
## Inspire Teachers

## JAHKARI H. TAYLOR

1. Teacher 2. Education. I Title. II. Title: Overcoming burnout: daily devotionals to inspire teachers.

Published in the United States of America.

# OVERCOMING

# BURNOUT

By Jahkari H. Taylor

www.purposepushers.com

# INVITATION

Before we embark on this journey to overcome burnout, I want to first invite you to accept Jesus Christ as your Lord and Savior. I truly believe overcoming burnout is impossible without Jesus Christ. Only He can fill you with the passion and purpose you have been searching for. Only He can encourage you daily and give you the strength you will need to teach in today's schools. Only He can continuously remind you of the reason you decided to answer the call to be a teacher in the first place. You really did not choose to teach, teaching chose you. It was destiny.

When you evaluate Jesus' life, you will see an awesome testament of destiny. In addition, when we read about what He had to endure, we quickly realize that stepping into destiny can be uncomfortable. It can be painful and exhausting because of the pressures that accompany the purpose. Yet, at the same time Jesus shows us that it is possible to find fulfillment while experiencing the pressures of purpose. Despite the mental, physical, and emotional discomfort that He experienced, He never gave up. He endured every obstacle because He understood that He was on a divine assignment. Now, I do not know where you are in the process of overcoming burnout but you need to know that you too are on a divine assignment for God. So, why not accept the invitation today and allow Jesus to help you along this journey.

# DEDICATION

This book is dedicated to all of my colleagues, friends and fellow educators who desire to make a difference in the lives of young people each day. Whether you are a bus driver, cafeteria worker, custodian, substitute teacher, office worker, school nurse, security, teacher assistant, teacher, guidance counselor, school social worker, administrator, or anyone else who works in schools, I dedicate this book to you. Your efforts do not go unnoticed. You are valuable and appreciated for your selfless service. Thank you for all that you do.

# CONTENTS

# ACKNOWLEDGMENTS

First and foremost, I have to thank God for His steadfast love and faithful presence in my life. Without God, nothing that I do would be possible or meaningful.

I also have to thank God for my lovely wife, Shalise. My wife is my life partner, my chief supporter, and my inspiration. My wife is by my side on the battlefields of ministry as well as the battlefields of education. Thank you for your perseverance and love, baby. I love you dearly.

I want to acknowledge my four children, Jahkari, Jaden, Jayla, and Josiah who are truly blessings from God. My children are some of the greatest teachers I've ever had. And to my mother who was my first teacher, I thank you for everything you have taught and instilled in me. I love you.

Thank you also to my Oscar F. Smith High School family. You guys truly embody the type of grit and determination needed in every school. Keep the faith and keep fighting!

# REAL-LIFE TEACHER STORIES

**Mrs. Johnson, a Music teacher of 27 years, stated:**

*"I am so glad that I only have 3 years left before I retire. The field of education has changed so much since my first year. Nowadays, teachers are practically responsible for raising their students. The only thing we can't do is claim them as dependents on our taxes but we are expected to do everything else for them."*

**Mr. Martinez, a Math teacher of 6 years, stated:**

*"I've already applied for 4 jobs outside of teaching because I can make a whole lot more money if I switch careers. Not to mention, I will be a lot less stressed. It's not even the students that get to me; it's their parents. Some parents contact me every other day and then they get angry when I do not respond to their emails immediately. They've even tried to report me to my principal behind these issues. I do not have to tolerate this type of stress. As soon as a door opens up for me, I'm gone."*

**Ms. Sanders, a Science teacher of 9 years, stated:**

*"I am a single parent trying to be a strong mother and an effective teacher but this is no easy task. Some days, I have to catch myself because the frustration that begins at school can sometimes follow me all the way home. Sometimes I find myself taking my frustrations from work out on my own children. One day my son said, 'Mommy can we go to the park' and I snapped at him as if he raised his hand to hit me. It was just that I had a long day and I was tired."*

**Mrs. White, an English teacher of 14 years, stated:**

*"It seems as if each year gets worst. I feel as if I am swamped by unnecessary paperwork, disrespectful students, and administrators who provide absolutely no support. I can't keep coming back. I've had to take multiple days off this year just to rest and find peace. I am so frustrated."*

These stories represent the daily thought patterns of many educators across the world. They have arrived at a place of fatigue and exhaustion in the field of education. They desire to teach and make a difference in the lives of their students but at the same time they have contemplated leaving the profession altogether at one point or another. These teachers are struggling with teacher "burn out" and they desperately need to find inspiration on a personal level.

The good news is there is a remedy to help teachers overcome the dreaded feeling that burnout brings. I pray that everyone who reads this book will find the inspiration that is needed to overcome burnout.

# INTRODUCTION

If anyone understands the power of reading books it's educators. In the world of education reading is truly fundamental. You will most likely find books in every school, in almost every classroom. They represent essential and necessary educational tools. Yet, on the outside of school there are some people who refuse to see the value of books and they certainly refuse to believe books have the potential to change lives. For me, books are therapeutic and I personally believe the right types of books can transform lives.

In today's libraries there are many different types of book genres, including the following: science fiction, horror, history, health, education, mystery, romance, and self-help, just to name a few. Each book has the potential to change the way we perceive ourselves and the world we live in. Some books can even help us change the way we view our jobs. Personally, I have never read a book (outside of the Bible) that changed my perception of my career as a teacher. In fact, I am sure that I have never picked up a book that contained educational and spiritual insight, specifically designed to help teachers overcome burnout.

Maybe this is due to the fact that this topic is extremely specific. Maybe these types of books do not abound because people think God has no place in education. Maybe this is due to the fact that many authors have never been school teachers or maybe this is due to the fact that people believe spirituality belongs in its own separate "religious box." I really do not know why books that apply Christian theological principles to everyday life do not abound to the degree of self-help books, but I would assume that this is simply the result of a world that places more trust in a limited man than an all-powerful God.

As a public-school teacher, I can assure you that I need a lot more than self-help books in order to be effective in my profession. Self-help books are good, but they cannot help me maintain peace of mind. Personally, I need God if I want to maintain my sanity. I honestly desire to know how anyone could maintain peace in cramped classrooms, filled with diverse groups of highly expressive and needy children without the help of God.

How is it possible to manage students' behaviors, plan lessons, grade papers, hold conferences, develop assessments, and prepare students for high pressured standardized tests without God? How can people do all of these things, then go home to manage their own household, nurture their own children, and handle their own personal issues while at the same time maintaining peace? Do I also need to mention the salary most teachers are living off of? I think you get the picture... Teachers need God. I do not think it is possible to approach each day with purpose and passion in today's schools without supernatural assistance.

If teachers are to overcome burnout, God will have to play a major role in their lives. Burnout is not Mr. Nice Guy. It is a debilitating condition that has the potential to suck the life out of the most energetic, passionate, and determined professionals. It can lead to physical symptoms such as headaches, diseases, and other stress-induced illnesses. So, for the sake of your own mental, physical, and emotional health, you must overcome burnout.

Although this book relates to most working-professionals, the content is narrowly focused on inspiring educators to overcome burnout on their jobs. There are a total of six sections throughout the book. Each section contains a positive affirmation that should be declared each morning before the school day begins for at least one week. In addition, each section contains a school weeks' worth of devotionals that are designed to help educators embrace the correct perspective of their job in order to overcome burnout. There is no quick fix to overcoming burnout because it is a continuous process of changing the way you see yourself and your job on a daily basis. Therefore, it is a never-ending journey. The good news is... There are many people, like you, who are willing to begin the journey to overcome burnout. So, let's begin the journey together.

# QUESTION

## Are You "Burnt Out?"

Professor and Director of Clinical Training in the Department of Psychology at Rutgers University, Dr. Maurice J. Elias, believes there are some significant warning signs that a person can look for to determine if they are in fact "burnt out." He suggests answering the following questions:

1. "Do you feel run down and drained of physical or emotional energy?
2. Do you find that you are prone to negative thinking about your job?
3. Do you find that you are harder and less sympathetic with people than perhaps they deserve?
4. Do you find yourself getting easily irritated by small problems, or by your co-workers and team?
5. Do you feel misunderstood or unappreciated by your co-workers?
6. Do you feel that you have no one to talk to?
7. Do you feel an unpleasant level of pressure to succeed?
8. Do you feel that you are not getting what you want out of your job?

9.  Do you feel that you are in the wrong organization or the wrong profession?

10. Are you becoming frustrated with parts of your job?

11. Do you feel that organizational politics or bureaucracy frustrate your ability to do a good job?"[i]

If you have answered yes to all or any of the aforementioned questions, today is a good day to start putting forth an intentional effort toward overcoming burnout.  So, the question is… Where do you start?  I recommend that you begin the process of overcoming burnout by using the Bible to direct your thoughts.

# ANSWER

## Change Your Mind

**Romans 12:2 (NIV)**

*"Do not conform to the pattern of this world, but be transformed by the renewing of your mind."*

In the Bible the word "transformed" is translated from the Greek word "metamorphoo."[ii] This term, "metamorphoo" is where we derive our English term "metamorphosis," which refers to a transformation or change. I believe everyone desires a change for the better. Everyone is always looking to change from a lesser state to a more advanced state, from a state of frustration to a state of peace, from a state of emptiness to a state of fulfillment. Teachers and other professionals who feel burnt out are definitely searching for this type of change. Whether it is a change in careers or a change from thought patterns that lead to burn out, one thing is certain: Change is always being considered. If you are truly ready for a change, start to focus your energy and efforts on intentional thinking. Concentrate on taking control of your own thoughts by renewing your mind.

The biblical word "Renew" was translated from an earlier Greek word that means "renovate."[iii] Renovate as in "out with the old and in with the new." Get those negative, pessimistic, deflating, self-defeating thoughts out of your head! Renovate your mind by removing your own thoughts and inserting God's thoughts. You can find God's thoughts in God's Word, the Holy Bible. So, go ahead… Dust your Bible off right now and start reading. Only then will you begin the process of overcoming burnout.

### Prayer

*Heavenly Father, remind me to look to you to draw strength, passion, and purpose. Change my mind and my heart as you inspire me to overcome burnout.*

# SECTION 1 AFFIRMATION

## "I Am a Teacher with a Purpose!"

**Philippians 4:13 (NASB)**

*"I can do all things through Him who strengthens me"*

## Practical Realization

Teaching is very similar to rock climbing. It requires strength, toughness, determination, and tremendous focus. One distraction or misstep can be very difficult to recover from. Therefore, concentration is essential. Do not allow anything or anyone to distract you from the task at hand. Stay focused on success, no matter how distant it may appear to be. As you keep climbing you will realize that success is not as far away as it once appeared. However, it is totally up to you to keep climbing despite your fatigue. Let's get started!

# Day 1: The Divine Origin of Teaching

## Exodus 4:12 (NKJV)

*"Now therefore, go, and I will be with your mouth and teach you what you shall say."*

The first time the word "teach" is ever used in the Bible occurs in the book of Exodus. In this context, God is instructing Moses to fulfill his divine purpose by leading the Children of Israel out of slavery in Egypt. However, after God commissioned Moses to lead the people out of bondage, Moses began to voice resistance and apprehension because of his own personal insecurities. Can you believe one of the greatest leaders of all time initially lacked the confidence to fulfill his own purpose! So how did he find the courage he needed to fulfill his purpose?

After Moses expressed a lack of self-confidence, God gives him some words of encouragement by promising to "teach" him what he should do in order to fulfill his purpose. What a powerful understanding of teaching! Teaching would be all Moses would need to fulfill his purpose, overcome his personal insecurities, and live with confidence. Over the last ten years as an educator, I have learned that Moses is not the only person who needs effective teaching in order to overcome personal insecurities. Like Moses, all students have tremendous potential but they all need effective teaching to help them access the God-given greatness that's on the inside.

All students require effective teaching in order to fulfill their purpose in life. These facts highlight the significance of teaching and the role of teachers in human development. As you seek to teach people regardless of their age, ethnicity, or background, always remain conscious of the power of teaching. Remember, you have the opportunity to help develop a confident leader who can truly make a difference in this world. The teaching that Moses received helped him earn the reputation as one of the greatest leaders in biblical history. So, never underestimate the power of good teaching!

### Prayer

*Heavenly Father, empower me and guide me as I seek to teach my students to continually strive to reach their God-given potential. Amen.*

# Day 2: Compassionate Teacher

## Matthew 9:36 (NLT)

*"When he saw the crowds, he had compassion on them because they were confused and helpless, like sheep without a shepherd."*

Jesus Christ is undoubtedly the greatest, most influential teacher to ever walk the face of this planet. The teachings that He left behind have continued to transcend time, language, and cultural boundaries. He was fully God and fully man, which means He was definitely more advantaged than all of us but we can still learn a great deal from His teachings and His teaching philosophy. Jesus was the epitome of a passionate teacher. He always captivated His audience and maintained their attention without the use of modern gadgets, such as wireless microphones and smart board technologies. Most people were captivated by His teachings because of His sheer compassion for people. Everyone has heard of the passion of Christ but the Bible also provides countless illustrations of the compassion of Christ.

Compassion is an emotional connection that inspires action. It is a feeling of deep sympathy and sorrow that subtly moves us to do what we can to alleviate the suffering and misfortune of others. Compassionate teachers will always captivate and maintain the attention of their students because students interpret compassion as love. When students feel loved by a teacher, they will do almost anything to please that teacher. This includes showing respect, completing homework, and studying to pass tests. These are just a few by-products that result from a student who senses the presence of a compassionate teacher. If you desire to reach your students, start by communicating compassion through your actions.

Compassionate teachers realize that students may come in all shapes, sizes, and ages but at the end of the day every student is a child who needs help. Some need academic help, some need emotional help, and some simply need all the help they can get. As a teacher, you possess all the characteristics and skills necessary to meet the unique needs of all of your students. Now you need the type of compassion that will inspire you to help all students, even those that you would consider to be the most challenging.

**Prayer**

*Heavenly Father, I pray that you will stir the compassion within my heart and inspire me to do all that I can to help my students. Amen.*

# Day 3: The Great Commission to Teach

## Matthew 28:18-20 (NASB)

*"And Jesus came up and spoke to them, saying, 'All authority has been given to Me in heaven and on earth. Go therefore, and make disciples of all the nations, baptizing them in the name of the Father and the Son and the Holy Spirit, teaching them to observe all that I commanded you; and lo, I am with you always, even to the end of the age."*

No doubt, Jesus lived to fulfill His purpose on earth and teaching was a significant part of that purpose. It took Him 33 years to complete the task but He was determined to fulfill His purpose. During His lifetime He experienced opposition from the Roman government, rejection from the religious community, and even betrayal from someone He called His "Friend." Yet, in spite of the opposition He experienced, He remained committed to His mission.

Throughout His three-year ministry He demonstrated tremendous grit by holding firm to His commitment to teach His disciples how to fulfill their purpose. After He was crucified on a rugged Roman cross, His lifeless body was placed in a tomb. After three days He rose from the grave, alive, with all power in His hands! He then proceeded to appear to all of His disciples with the intent of teaching His last lesson on earth. Before He left, He desired to give His disciples the most important assignment of their lives. He basically told them to go into all nations and work tirelessly as teachers! Literally, He said, "Go therefore, and make disciples of all nations."

The word "disciple" used in this context is derived from the earlier Greek word "mathetes,"[iv] which refers to "a learner, a disciple, or a pupil." In other words, Jesus commissioned His disciples to go into the world and train learners, which means they were dispatched to be teachers. What a great honor bestowed upon all who would answer the call to teach!

### Prayer

*Heavenly Father, I pray for the correct understanding of my purpose as a teacher. I recognize the stress and frustration that accompanies this calling and I ask for Christ-like patience and strength to teach in spite of the challenges.*

# Day 4: "I Am Here for You"

## Psalm 32:8 (NIV)

*"I will instruct you and teach you in the way you should go; I will counsel you with my loving eye on you."*

King David of Israel, who is well-known as the boy who killed the giant with a slingshot, is credited with writing this Psalm. Alluding to God's compassionate and loving care, King David expressed the great joy of knowing God would instruct him, teach him, and counsel him with a loving eye. I have found that most people, especially students, desire to express the same joy of knowing that someone cares for them. All students are looking for a teacher who will instruct them, teach them, and counsel them with a loving eye.

Yet, most students have never heard teachers utter words of personal interest and genuine concern for their well-being as people. They are accustomed to hearing direct instruction and correction. They are also accustomed to hearing the curriculum being communicated with passion. However, when it comes to hearing words of endearment, students feel most teachers are silent. Some teachers may feel that using words of endearment may hinder their ability to discipline students. Yet, this is a flawed perspective. Most students will gladly receive correction from teachers who balance discipline with words of endearment. The fact of the matter is, sometimes students need to hear these direct words of affection from the lips of their teachers: "I am here for you."

## Prayer

*Heavenly Father, help me to genuinely communicate words of endearment and affection to my students. I also ask you to help them understand that I am here for them. Amen.*

# Day 5: "No Immediate Fruits!"

## Matthew 13:3-9 (NIV)

*Then he told them many things in parables, saying: "A farmer went out to sow his seed. As he was scattering the seed, some fell along the path, and the birds came and ate it up. Some fell on rocky places, where it did not have much soil. It sprang up quickly, because the soil was shallow. But when the sun came up, the plants were scorched, and they withered because they had no root. Other seed fell among thorns, which grew up and choked the plants. Still other seed fell on good soil, where it produced a crop—a hundred, sixty or thirty times what was sown. Whoever has ears, let them hear."*

One day when Jesus sat by a lake He taught this parable to large crowds. This parable contains theological and spiritual truths about how people respond to the Gospel message. To summarize the main point about what Jesus was teaching we can conclude with this: "The condition of your heart will ultimately dictate what you allow to take root in it." Jesus attempted to spread the Word of God throughout His 33 years of life but not everyone received it. Some people blatantly and forcefully rejected what he taught.

As a teacher, there will be days when you have a similar experience. There will be days when your students completely disregard what you are teaching. Some days it may feel as if you are scattering seed on a path that does not contain fertile soil. This is usually evidenced by poor tests scores which may indicate that we have completely missed the mark with our instruction. There will also be days when it seems like you are scattering seed on rocky places. This occurs when students shake their heads as if they understand what is being taught but in all reality, nothing took root. In addition, there may be times when it seems like you are scattering seed among thorns. This occurs when you are trying to teach but distractions and disruptions prevent progress.

When these moments of adversity occur, you will sense the presence of teacher burnout trying to creep into your thoughts. Yet, you cannot give in to it. You must keep sowing! Keep scattering the seed of your instruction until it falls on the fertile soil of your students' minds. Only then will your instruction produce a harvest. In order to find the motivation you need to keep sowing, keep this simple truth at the forefront of your mind: "There is no such thing as immediate fruit." Harvest is the product of preparing the soil, watering the soil, and planting the seed. Then the last key ingredient is patience.

# Prayer

*Heavenly Father, give me the endurance to persevere with patience as I strive to provide effective and meaningful instruction.  I also ask you to give my students a teachable spirit and a desire to learn.*

# SECTION 1 REVIEW & APPLY

Explain which Bible verse from this section has helped you the most and why.

_____

_____

_____

_____

_____

Which prayer from this section has helped you the most and why?

_____

_____

_____

_____

_____

How will you apply what you have read this week?

_____

_____

_____

_____

_____

**Go to overcomingburnout.com and share your insight with the larger community!**

# SECTION 2 AFFIRMATION

## "I Am a Coordinator of Compassion!"

**Psalm 103:4 (NIV)**

*"As a father has compassion on his children, so the Lord has compassion on those who fear him"*

## Practical Realization

Compassion is much like empathy in the sense that it involves vicariously experiencing the feelings, thoughts or attitudes of another. When compassion works in the heart of the teacher, it challenges the teacher to exhaust all creative abilities just to reach all students. It will allow a teacher to notice that one student in the classroom who needs help but refuses to ask for assistance. Compassionate teachers see struggling students and refuse to sit idly as these students slip into the abyss of hopelessness and failure. Compassion causes teachers to empathize with the students who appear to be hanging on by a thread. Therefore, all compassionate teachers will put themselves in a position to pull students up with a helping hand because of the compassion in their hearts.

# Day 6: "We're All in it Together"

**Psalm 133:1 (NKJV)**

*"Behold, how good and how pleasant it is for brethren to dwell together in unity!"*

The word "unity" implies oneness, harmony, and agreement. Many people would agree that unity is necessary if any relationship is to be healthy and sustainable. However, unity is unfortunately a rare commodity in our world today. It is not something that is portrayed consistently on television, radio, or other forms of mass media. In fact, many would argue that unity has been an elusive concept since the beginning of time, which means young people have unfortunately inherited a divided and divisive world.

With this reality, teachers have the arduous task of creating a counter-culture in their classrooms. Teachers must develop a classroom culture where every child feels as if he or she belongs. No doubt, this will be quite a challenge considering the great diversity within our schools today, but it is mandatory if all students are expected to experience academic success. Linda Albert, a counselor, university professor, former teacher, and author of *Cooperative Discipline*, believes "Belonging and

Cooperation" are two vital components of education.[v] Albert believes classroom success will depend heavily upon a teacher's ability or willingness to develop students' sense of connectedness.

Obviously, connectedness and unity are interrelated. Teachers will need both in order to eliminate bullying and reduce unhealthy competition in the classroom. This will require lessons that encourage students to work together despite their differences. Teachers will have a major role to play in this process because students naturally develop cliques with individuals who they feel are most similar to themselves. A concerted effort must be put forth on behalf of the teacher to ensure that students do not feel marginalized or excluded.

Over the last two decades, we have all witnessed the devastating and detrimental impact that exclusive in-groups have had on young minds. We have witnessed countless school shootings and suicidal behaviors that resulted from particular students who felt as if they did not "fit in." Therefore, it is mandatory for educators to create an atmosphere in their classroom that increases collaboration and group interdependence. Students need to know "We're all in this together."

# Prayer

*Heavenly Father, I pray that you will use me to create an atmosphere of collaboration in my classroom where all students feel a sense of belonging. Help my students achieve unity despite their differences. Amen.*

# Day 7: Love is in the Air

## 1 John 4:18 (NKJV)

*"There is no fear in love; but perfect love casts out fear."*

Many people consider love to be one of the most powerful forces on the planet. Love can cause a person to do almost anything, which makes love one of the greatest motivators in our world. This is due, in part, to the fact that love provides a sense of freedom and security that is necessary to the human psyche. Love completely removes fear. How many parents have witnessed their children jump into their arms without fear because they knew their loving parent would catch them? I can recall one such situation where my four-year-old daughter jumped from the sixth step in my house because she believed I would catch her. She did it without warning too. She didn't even say, "Daddy catch me!" She just jumped and thank God I caught her.

She jumped because she was motivated by love and I caught her because I was also motivated by love. I believe love can motivate students in the classroom to jump into the unknown potential of their mental capacities. I also believe love can motivate students to step outside of their comfort zones and pursue success without fear of failure because love, by nature, will provide the sense of freedom and security they need to thrive. Love is a safe place. When students enter a classroom atmosphere of love, they do not have to be fearful or anxious of failure.

When love is in the air, students feel protected from the belittlement that has a tendency to result from making mistakes. Many students do not want to try because they are afraid to fail. They do not want to deal with the possibility of being ridiculed for making a mistake. Therefore, they will preserve their dignity at all costs, even if it means refusing to participate. Many students will even refuse to comply with a reasonable request to read out loud because they fear ridicule may result from the mispronunciation of a word. Yet, when love is in the air students have the liberty to make mistakes that are essential to the learning process. By creating an atmosphere of love in the classroom, teachers can establish a safe space for all students.

### Prayer

*Heavenly Father, teach me how to love so I may model it in every area of my life, especially in my classroom. Show me how to create an atmosphere of love where all my students can feel safe. Amen.*

# Day 8: Short-term Memory

## Colossians 3:13 (NLT)

*"Make allowance for each other's faults, and forgive anyone who offends you."*

Teaching is not a science. It is a creative and expressive form of art. If it is to be effective, teaching cannot be reduced to cold-hearted facts and neither can it be simplified to merely managing people. Effective teaching will always be the purest form of leadership. It involves using skill and influence to guide students in the direction toward fulfilling their potential. Therefore, as with leadership, teachers must rely heavily on modeling appropriate behaviors and work habits.

Through modeling, teachers have the ability to teach crucial life lessons. One life lesson that teachers will frequently have the opportunity to teach through modeling is forgiveness. Every teacher will be offended or disrespected at some point in time. There will always be students who direct their frustration and anger toward teachers. So, what do you do when a student offends you? What do you do when you conclude that a particular student is trying to intentionally irritate you? I challenge you to muster up enough strength to demonstrate forgiveness.

During these heated moments, you will have a perfect opportunity to teach students the invaluable trait of forgiveness. However, you must be careful not to teach students to become vindictive, spiteful, and bitter through your actions. Always take the higher road, no matter how you feel, because your students are watching and taking mental notes of how you handle conflict. They will one day be in a similar situation and they may put into practice what they have learned from your role modeling. In some cases, it may be wise to explicitly state, "I realize that you desire to challenge me because you are upset and frustrated. I understand completely but when you calm down, I want you to know that I forgive you for your behavior."

## Prayer

*Heavenly Father, give me the strength to demonstrate forgiveness. I know that harboring feelings of resentment toward my students will hinder my ability to reach them and teach them. Therefore, I ask that you will grant me short-term memory so I can start fresh each day. Amen.*

# Day 9: Sticks and Stones

**Proverbs 18:21 (NKJV)**

*"Death and life are in the power of the tongue."*

Growing up as a child can be brutal, especially when you have to deal with bullies. When I was picked on as a child, I would tell my mother and she would always say, "Sticks and stones may break your bones but words will never harm you." I think my mother believed these words would comfort me and for a moment they did. However, when I left from my mother's presence, I realized her words were unable to remove the emotional pain and discomfort that I felt from the hurtful words directed at me. Now, as an adult, I realize that my mother's words were not as true as I once thought. In fact, now I believe the opposite to be true. Sticks and stones do not hurt as much as words.

According to Bullyingstatistics.org, "There is a strong link between bullying and suicide."[vi] Bullying victims are between 2 and 9 times more likely to consider suicide than non-victims, according to studies by Yale University.[vii] The statistics indicate that suicide is the third leading cause of death among young people. In addition, it has been reported that for every suicide among young people there are at least 100 attempts.[viii]

With these grim statistics, teachers have no other choice but to be more vigilant and alert to the communication taking place in their classrooms. Teachers should listen attentively to verbal communication in the class while also looking for non-verbal signs as well. In fact, it would be prudent for teachers to convey clear and concise parameters for communication within the learning environment. Students need to know exactly what is acceptable and what is out of bounds as it relates to classroom communication. The sad epidemic of bullying is proof that death and life are in the power of the tongue. Every person has the power to encourage or discourage, to build up or tear down and school should be a place where young minds are constructed, not demolished.

## Prayer

*Heavenly Father, help me to become more in tune with my students. I pray that my classroom will be a place of peace, comfort, and security. Amen.*

# Day 10: Communicating Love

## 1 Corinthians 13:1 (NLT)

*"If I could speak all the languages of earth and of angels but didn't love others, I would only be a noisy gong or a clanging cymbal."*

Communication is arguably the most important of all life skills. It involves sharing and exchanging information, ideas, and feelings. It not only involves speech and language but also non-verbal cues and gestures. When we fail in the area of communication, all forward progression arrives at a standstill. This is true in our relationships, in our families, and also in our classrooms.

For these reasons, one of our main goals in life should involve becoming a more effective communicator. The reality is, no one benefits from failed communication, mixed messages, and unintended signals. Can you imagine the traffic light sending mixed signals? What if the traffic light signaled a green light when it should indicate a red light? Obviously, this would not be good. This same understanding can be applied to the field of teaching. So, what signals are you sending in your classroom? Sometimes it's not what you say, but it's how you say it.

This is why all teachers should continually strive to improve in the area of communication.

I have learned that students are constantly analyzing teachers to see if they are communicating love. Students do not care if teachers hold more degrees than thermometers. The only thing they want to know is… Are you sending genuine signals of compassion? Does this curriculum contain any love? Is this lesson going to connect with me? In the eyes of most students, a teacher who has a mind full of curriculum with a heart empty of love is devoid of any real substance. So, communicate content that contains love.

**Prayer**

*Heavenly Father, I pray for the ability to communicate love to my students. I also ask that you will open my students' hearts so they will know that I care for them. Amen.*

# SECTION 2 REVIEW & APPLY

Explain which Bible verse from this section has helped you
the most and why.

_____

_____

_____

_____

_____

Which prayer from this section has helped you the most
and why?

_____

_____

_____

_____

_____

How will you apply what you have read this week?

_____

_____

_____

_____

_____

**Go to <u>overcomingburnout.com</u> and share your insight with the
larger community!**

# SECTION 3 AFFIRMATION

## "I Am a Facilitator of Learning!"

### Hebrews 12:1 (NLT)

*"Therefore, since we are surrounded by such a huge crowd of witnesses to the life of faith, let us strip off every weight that slows us down, especially the sin that so easily trips us up. And let us run with endurance the race that God has set before us."*

## Practical Realization

Facilitating learning is much like participating in sports. Yet, of all the different types of athletes that exist, I believe track and field hurdlers have much in common with teachers. As the umpire prepares to shout, "On your mark, get set, go!" The hurdler is already contemplating the finish line. She is focused and determined to run the race successfully. Fully aware of what lies ahead, she embraces the challenge with confidence. She knows that there is a possibility of being completely exhausted and maybe even failing in the process. She is also aware of the obstacles that stand in her way but yet she is already mentally prepared to get over every hurdle. She must maintain concentration and focus in order to get across the finish line. Teaching is much like that. The only difference between the teacher and the hurdler is the distance they have to travel. The hurdler's race is much more of a sprint, whereas the teacher's should be considered a marathon. Nevertheless, both must run with patience. Get ready, get set, go!

# Day 11: Self-Assessment

**Proverbs 1:2-3 (NKJV)**

*"To know wisdom and instruction, to perceive the words of understanding, to receive the instruction of wisdom, justice, judgment, and equity;"*

As a facilitator of learning, a teacher has one ultimate goal: deliver effective instruction. Nothing can serve as a substitute for good, quality instruction. We can debate pedagogy and methodology all day long but the desired result of teaching is not up for debate. The end result of teaching should always be learning. At the end of each lesson, teachers should ask themselves: What did my students learn? Did any of my students fail to grasp the lesson? Can my students prove that they have learned what I attempted to teach? These are the types of questions all facilitators of learning must ask themselves.

Self-assessments will always be the best assessments for teachers and students. Through honest self-evaluations, teachers can use their findings to make necessary adjustments to their lessons and delivery methods. These adjustments can help to ensure quality instruction is being facilitated. I encourage you to assess your students regularly but assess yourself most frequently. This will ensure that learning is taking place.

## Prayer

*Heavenly Father, as I seek to achieve my full potential as a facilitator of learning, I pray that you will help me engage in honest introspection each day.  Amen.*

# Day 12: Mastering the Art

**Proverbs 1:4-5 (NKJV)**

*"To give prudence to the simple, to the young man knowledge and discretion. A wise man will hear and increase learning, and a man of understanding will attain wise counsel."*

Most teachers do not get to handpick the type of students they will teach. In fact, the first day of class is somewhat of a mystery for most teachers. Teachers show up on day one and immediately notice that all of their students are different. Some students are quick learners; some are average, while others may learn at a slower pace. Some are energetic and extroverted, while others may be reserved and quiet. The great diversity in classrooms of today is a beautiful thing, but it makes teaching a bit more complex than it was in the past. In some cases, just when a teacher feels as if he or she knows the type of students in his or her class, the students prove themselves to be ever-changing, ever-evolving, and maturing as the year progresses. Yet, despite the capricious nature of students and their unique differences, the teacher is still tasked with teaching all students effectively.

The best teachers in every school can effectively facilitate learning and generate results with a diverse group of students who have different learning needs. Almost all educators of today have heard of the concept referred to as "Differentiated Instruction." The leading voice for differentiated instruction, Dr. Carol Tomlinson, defines it with these words: "The idea of differentiating instruction is an approach to teaching that advocates active planning for and attention to student differences in classrooms, in the context of high-quality curriculums."[ix] Differentiated instruction is all about accounting for the unique needs of all students.

Although this concept seems like a common sense approach to modern education, very few teachers actually differentiate instruction. This is primarily due to the fact that many people view differentiated instruction as merely a political buzzword, opposed to a valid educational philosophy. Nonetheless, in order to master the art of teaching, educators have to educate all learners by differentiating instruction and utilizing a variety of teaching modalities.

### Prayer

*Heavenly Father, help me to have a heart for all students and not just the ones who are the easiest to teach. Give me the ability to teach all students effectively. Amen.*

# Day 13: Better than Before

**Proverbs 9:9 (NKJV)**

*"Give instruction to a wise man and he will be still wiser;*
*teach a just man and he will increase in learning."*

Every teacher desires to make a positive and permanent impression upon his or her students. We all want to be assured that our students will be better than they were before because they have taken our class. If a student's reading ability is considered to be a 5 out of 10 on the first day of class, we all hope that he or she will, at the very minimum, be a 6 out of 10 by the time he or she leaves our class. If a student despises the particular subject area we teach, we would hope to, at least, help the student develop a more favorable opinion by the time he or she leaves our class. Simply put, we want our students to be better than before because of our presence.

It would be unrealistic to think all of our students will share the same passion we have for the content we teach just because they have sat in our classrooms. Yet, it is not unreasonable for all of our students to improve in the subject area that we teach because they had us as their teacher. So, set realistic goals for helping your students make incremental improvements. You may want to start by aiming to help them become more welcoming to your specific content. Then progressively move to helping students increase in knowledge about your content area. This will ensure that all of your students are, at the very minimal, better than before simply because they had you as their teacher.

## Prayer

*Heavenly Father, use me to help my students learn more about the content I teach. Also, help me to make a positive and long-lasting impact on my students so they will ultimately be better than before because they had my class. Amen.*

# Day 14: Catalyst of Hope

**Proverbs 3:13 (NKJV)**

*"Happy is the man who finds wisdom, And the man who gains understanding."*

Education has the power to change the world. It can break the devastating cycle of poverty, shape the next world leader, or empower a doctor to discover the cure for cancer. In addition, education can help individuals make more informed choices in their everyday lives. It can help people improve their personal health and wellness, while also improving social behaviors and attitudes in society. According to the Institute of Public Health in Ireland, greater levels of education can lead to "more opportunities for social development and enhanced social skills, with positive impacts for both the individual and the wider community, and subsequently, for general health."[x]

If education has the power to change lives, then educators are true catalysts for transforming entire communities. One educator who is committed to teaching with a purpose may not only make a difference in the life of a student but also may play a crucial role in the transformation of an entire family. It is also well-documented that individuals with more education have a longer life expectancy and live with less stress than those with less education. This is due to a host a factors but most notable are the economic opportunities that accompany education. More education usually leads to higher incomes and expanded social networks. Many of these social networks bring access to variety of different resources that also lead to better outcomes. Therefore, the research supports the biblical view that affirms, "Happy is the man who finds wisdom, and the man who gains understanding." Day by day, teachers are helping to transform individuals, families, and communities.

## Prayer

*Heavenly Father, help me to understand the true power of my presence and influence as a teacher. I pray that you will help me to realize the impact that I can make on my students as a catalyst of hope and transformation. Amen.*

# Day 15: Do you Understand?

**Proverbs 4:7 (NKJV)**

*"Wisdom is the principal thing; therefore get wisdom. And in all your getting, get understanding."*

Vocabulary is significant in every language, especially the biblical languages of Hebrew, Aramaic, and Greek. In the earliest biblical language, Hebrew, the word "wisdom" referred to "skill" whereas the word "understanding" referred to "the act or application of wisdom" which is skill. Wisdom is good but what good is wisdom that is unapplied! What good is it to possess knowledge but never act on the knowledge you possess?

If educators were to apply the Hebrew concept of "understanding" to education today, we would have to conclude that a student has not learned the content being taught until he or she can demonstrate what they have learned through application. Maybe this Hebrew concept is finally resurfacing itself in the modern educational experience under the guise of "rigor." Rigor is touted as challenging and demanding instruction that helps students elevate their own expectations and academic performances.[xi]

Many of the latest standardized assessments contain rigor in the form of virtual manipulatives that require students to "drag and drop" or interact with the assessments to prove that they know what they are doing. These rigorous assessments go beyond circling a multiple choice answer and are believed to be the most accurate and reliable assessments. Through these types of assessments students have the opportunity to demonstrate their ability to act on and apply what they have previously learned. This means teachers of the next generation must be ready to ensure that students get "understanding" above everything else.

**Prayer**

*Heavenly Father, give me the energy to invest more time in the assessments I create. I pray that you will help me develop rigorous assessments that will challenge my students to bring the best out of themselves. Amen.*

# SECTION 3 REVIEW & APPLY

Explain which Bible verse from this section has helped you
the most and why.

_____

_____

_____

_____

_____

Which prayer from this section has helped you the most
and why?

_____

_____

_____

_____

_____

How will you apply what you have read this week?

_____

_____

_____

_____

_____

**Go to underlineovercomingburnout.com and share your insight with the
larger community!**

# SECTION 4 AFFIRMATION

## "I Am a Cultivator of Character!"

**Psalms 37:23 (NKJV)**

*"The steps of a good man are ordered by the Lord, And He delights in his way."*

## Practical Realization

Arguably the most influential civil rights leader in world history, Martin Luther King Jr., had a lot to say about education. Dr. King once said, "The function of education is to teach one to think intensively and to think critically. Intelligence plus character- that is the goal of true education."[xii] Dr. King's educational philosophy was holistic. It was not founded on developing competence alone but also the development of character. As teachers we have to take the necessary steps to cultivate the character of this next generation. If we continue to undermine the importance of character education, we will only aid in the development of creative criminals, talented thugs, reasonable racists, and brilliant bigots. So, let's step up and cultivate the character of our students.

# Day 16: Developing Diligence

## Proverbs 6:6-9 (NLT)

*"Take a lesson from the ants, you lazybones. Learn from their ways and become wise! Though they have no prince or governor or ruler to make them work, they labor hard all summer, gathering food for the winter. But you, lazybones, how long will you sleep? When will you wake up?"*

Overcoming burnout requires adopting a totally new perspective. You will need a new perspective of your purpose as a teacher and an entirely new perspective of your students. For example, if a student decides to sleep during your class, it does not necessary mean he or she is unwilling to learn, nor does it mean he or she desires to be defiant. The sleeper may be "unconsciously" sending you a message to alert you of your boring lesson plan. Or maybe the sleeper is simply sending you the following non-verbal message: "I want to be successful but my work ethic won't let me."

Most teachers fully understand that teaching involves motivating students as well as challenging them academically. The academic component is easy when students are motivated but how do you teach when students are unmotivated?  Most teachers are aware of the fact that many students lack a diligent work ethic.  On a positive side, a lack of work ethic does not mean it cannot be developed.  Sometimes teachers can awaken students' potential by providing real-life examples of diligence and determination.  One example that has worked for me is the example provided by ants.  Ants may be small in stature but they possess a work ethic that is large and in charge.  They never take days off; they are always persistent.  Even when children decide to intentionally destroy ant hills, ants do not slip into a state of frustrated stagnation.  They simply begin to build again.  What an awesome example of diligence and determination!

I believe the work ethic of ants is a clear indication of their overall character.  As teachers, we have to be intentional about cultivating the character of our students.  Teachers can begin this process by establishing high expectations for all students from day one.  Then, and only then, will students begin to work toward the goal of self-improvement, which ultimately leads to good character.

## Prayer

*Heavenly Father, help me to develop my students in every area of their life.  Use me to stretch them socially, emotionally, and intellectually.  Give me the wisdom and strength to build their character. Amen.*

# Day 17: Genuine and Authentic

**Romans 12:9 (NLT)**

*"Don't just pretend to love others. Really love them."*

In a world where political correctness is promoted at all cost, genuine and authentic communication has become somewhat scarce. Adults have set the example and children have mimicked their behaviors. This is one of the reasons why so many young people struggle to express their ideas and opinions openly. No one is showing them how to be genuine and authentic. So, how can teachers lead students to express themselves honestly and appropriately in the school setting?

First, teachers must express themselves genuinely, authentically, and appropriately in the school setting. Teachers cannot pretend to care for all students, while secretly concealing indifference or apathy toward particular students. If you are going to cultivate the character of your students, you first must begin to cultivate your own character. This means no hidden biases in your heart! You must look at all students through the same lens: the lens of genuine love and compassion. All students must be viewed as reachable, worthy of dignity, and destined for success in spite of the unique challenges they present.

Once teachers set the example of genuine and authentic care for all people, students will demonstrate the same behaviors. They will begin to genuinely embrace the learning environment and everyone in it.

## Prayer

*Heavenly Father, show me how to be genuine and authentic. I pray that you will remove every barrier in my heart that may hinder my sincere expression of love and concern for all of my students. Amen.*

# Day 18: No "I" in T.E.A.M.

**Ecclesiastes 4:12 (NLT)**

*"A person standing alone can be attacked and defeated, but two can stand back to back and conquer. Three are even better, for a triple-braided cord is not easily broken"*

Sports has the ability to teach many life lessons that impact people in a positive way. The concepts of "team" and "teamwork," which are intrinsically connected to all sports, can help individuals achieve success in every area of life. The acronym for T.E.A.M. is often touted to mean "Together Everyone Accomplishes More." It involves a combined effort in which each person contributes to the overall group. Effective teamwork requires individuals to place their personal agendas aside to focus on the common goal of the group. This is exactly what is needed to achieve success in any learning environment.

Teachers who desire to create a bully-free and judgment-free classroom must encourage collaboration and teamwork among students. Group work can help students develop the social skills and interpersonal relationship skills that are necessary to succeed in our world today. Many teachers and researchers have now acknowledged the benefits of peer tutoring, which indicates that teamwork not only deserves a prominent place in sports but also in education.

## Prayer

*Heavenly Father, please help me engage my students in the learning process while simultaneously cultivating their character. I pray that you will give me the wisdom and understanding to increase collaboration and cooperation in my classroom. Amen.*

# Day 19: Mixed Messages

**Ecclesiastes 7:9 (NLT)**

*"Control your temper for anger labels you a fool"*

We have all heard the phrase, "Actions speak louder than words." This old adage speaks to the fact that non-verbal communication can say more about a person than his or her verbal communication. Students often have a difficult time understanding this concept. Students may use oppositional body language or invasive proximity by encroaching someone's personal space and never realize the problems presented by these behaviors. This is primarily due to the fact that students tend to think verbal communication is the only form of communication. This is evidenced by a student saying, "I didn't even do anything" when he or she is redirected for staring at other students in an uncomfortable manner.

Many students fail to realize that they communicate non-verbally more than they do verbally. Consider how students express their emotions. When they are upset or angry they rarely verbalize the fact that they are upset or angry, they simply frown their face, place their head on the desk, or use a frustrated tone of voice. These non-verbal forms of communication are instinctive and second nature.

73

This understanding of non-verbal and verbal communication should cause us to rethink students' behavior altogether.

Teachers have to help students understand what they are communicating unintentionally and subconsciously through their non-verbal communication. Non-verbal communication methods include the following: facial expressions, gestures, clothing styles, odors, etc. By elevating students' awareness of verbal and non-verbal communication, teachers can help students avoid sending mixed messages that may get them into trouble.

## Prayer

*Heavenly Father, help me view all behaviors as a form of communication. I pray that you will give me the wisdom to read between the lines to interpret my students' behavior correctly. Amen.*

# Day 20: Self-Discipline Predicts Success

**Proverbs 14:29 (NLT)**

*"People with understanding control their anger; a hot temper shows great foolishness."*

According to the American Heritage Dictionary of the English Language, the word "self-discipline" is defined as "Training and control of oneself and one's conduct, usually for personal improvement."[xiii] Self-discipline has recently surfaced in educational research as a key contributor to academic success. In fact, some researchers have indicated that "self-discipline appears to be a better predictor of academic gain than intelligence (as measured by an IQ test)."[xiv]

One of the reasons self-discipline is linked to predicting academic success is due to the fact that students who are self-disciplined usually exhibit less behavioral issues that may impede academic progress. These types of behavioral issues may include: inattention, impulsivity, defiance, and physical aggression, to name a few. These issues can be reduced and ultimately eliminated as students learn to practice self-discipline in school. Self-discipline is necessary to help students achieve long-term goals that require patience and endurance. Anyone who has matriculated through the traditional educational system will agree that success will require patient endurance.

This type of focus and determination requires a great degree of self-discipline. Yet, the question teachers must ask themselves is this: How can I help my students become more self-disciplined and self-determined in school? I suggest the following:

1. Teach students to develop short-term goals for themselves.
2. Teach students to identify distractions and bad habits that are barriers to their progress.
3. Teach students to develop and implement a daily schedule that will help them establish new habits.
4. Teach students to schedule a concrete time at the end of their day to reflect on the progress they have made throughout the day.

**Prayer**

*Heavenly Father, teach me how to develop my students' self-discipline and self-determination skills. I also ask that you help me model self-discipline and self-determination in my life. Amen.*

# SECTION 4 REVIEW & APPLY

Explain which Bible verse from this section has helped you
the most and why.

_____

_____

_____

_____

_____

Which prayer from this section has helped you the most
and why?

_____

_____

_____

_____

_____

How will you apply what you have read this week?

_____

_____

_____

_____

_____

**Go to** overcomingburnout.com **and share your insight with the
larger community!**

# SECTION 5 AFFIRMATION

## "I Am a Director of Destinies!"

### Proverbs 11:14 (NIV)

*"Without wise leadership, a nation falls: there is safety in having many advisers."*

## Practical Realization

In films, a director is responsible for making sure every component of the film runs smoothly. This requires that the director be intimately connected to every part of the movie-making process. From visualizing the script to giving specific directions to the cast, the director has to be immersed in all of the details. Like a director, a teacher has to be immersed in all of the details of teaching while also maintaining a personal connection with the students. The teacher has to visualize the outcomes of every lesson and provide specific instructions in order to ensure success. Just as the success of the movie depends heavily on the leadership ability of the director, so does the success of the students depend heavily on the leadership ability of the teacher.

# Day 21: Setting a Gritty Example

**Titus 2:7 (NLT)**

*"And you yourself must be an example to them by doing
good works of every kind. Let everything you do reflect the
integrity and seriousness of your teaching."*

For years, using examples has been the dominant
instructional strategy employed by teachers and for good
reason. By using examples teachers can explicitly show
students how theory is connected to practice. For example,
a biology teacher may be able to explain the structure of an
animal cell in great detail but most students will remain
oblivious until a concrete example or model is presented. It
is the same with mathematical equations. A math teacher
may be able to explain how to solve for "Y" in an algebraic
equation but most students will still require a concrete
example to fully comprehend what the teacher is attempting
to teach.

It is clear that examples bring much-needed clarity
to the instructional process. Teachers can provide
examples in the class, as well as set the example for the
class. By setting the example for appropriate behaviors
teachers can explicitly show students behavioral norms and
expectations that may be unclear to the student. Every

teacher should make it a priority to demonstrate honesty, integrity, and truthfulness. In addition, teachers should model the never-give-up attitude that is embodied in the concept called "grit."

Angela Lee Duckworth, MacArthur Foundation award winner and research psychologist, defines grit as "passion and perseverance for very long-term goals."[xv] Mrs. Duckworth affirms, "Grit is having stamina... Its living life like a marathon, not a sprint."[xvi] Many psychologists and educational researchers are arriving at the conclusion that grit is the true key to success. This apparent epiphany has led to a push toward teaching students to become "gritty" in school. Yet, as of today, there are no concrete guidelines or formulas to help teachers teach students how to demonstrate grit. Personally, I believe the best way for teachers to teach grit is to set a gritty example. This means teachers should demonstrate persistence, perseverance, and determination as role models for their students.

## Prayer

*Heavenly Father, give me the inspiration and motivation to model grit for my students. Help me to be the example of passion and perseverance that I expect my students to demonstrate. Amen.*

# Day 22: Shaping a Generation

## Proverbs 30:11 (NKJV)

*"There is a generation that curses its father, and does not bless its mother."*

According to The Center for Generational Kinetics, there are five generations that make up the current American society: Traditionalists or Silent Generation (born 1945 and before), Baby Boomers (born 1946 to 1964), Generation X (born 1965 to 1976), Millennials or Gen Y (born 1977 to 1995), and iGen, Gen Z or Centennials (born 1996 and later).[xvii]

Each generation is influenced by its own historical and cultural context. The cartoons and shows that pervade the television, the songs that dominate the radio, and the behavioral standards accepted by society influence each generation. In addition, each generation is shaped by the educators of their time. Therefore, teachers must always remain mindful of the fact that they have the potential to mold an entirely new generation. Many critics have described the most recent generation as lazy, entitled, and bad-mannered. Some have even gone so far to say this newest generation of young people are the worst in history. I do not believe this sentiment is true at all. I believe each generation requires guidance in order to channel their emotional energies in the right direction.

Instead of criticizing an entire generation, I encourage the generational critics to roll up their sleeves and help move young people forward toward success. During the 1990's, there was a popularized phrase which stated, "It takes a village to raise a child." If this is a true statement, my question is… What does it take to raise an entire generation? Obviously, more than a village. However, the task of raising an entire generation has been left primarily in the hands of parents and educators. Neither of which are fully equipped and resourced to accomplish the task before them. Nevertheless, we have to embrace the challenge and focus on shaping the next generation for the better.

### Prayer

*Heavenly Father, I pray that you will help me to be more in tune with this generation. Lead me as I lead them, mold me as I seek to mold them, and teach me as I strive to teach them. Amen.*

# Day 23: #YOLO

**Ecclesiastes 9:10 (NLT)**

*"Whatever you do, do well. For when you go to the grave, there will be no work or planning or knowledge or wisdom."*

The phrase "You only live once' has been popularized by singers, songwriters, and authors from all walks of life. That phrase has even taken on new form to a new generation that declares, "YOLO," which is an acronym for the popular phrase. Some may wonder how this phrase has continued to survive multiple generations and still maintain a high level of popularity. The answer is rooted in the truth that the phrase contains. You only live once on God's green earth and that is a statement of fact. Therefore, whatever you do, do it well.

Teachers can embrace this understanding and make it the classroom motto: "You only live once so give life your best shot!" You only attend high school once so put forth your best effort. Study for every test, work hard to complete every assignment, and strive to achieve every realistic goal you set for your life. Leave nothing unfinished because you only live once. No matter how morbid it may seem to talk about death, graveyards, and cemeteries, every living person will one day leave God's green earth.

So, why not give life all you have before you depart? Why not strive to achieve your potential in every area of your life before your time is up? All unused energy and all untapped potential will serve no purpose once our time is up. We need to understand this reality first and then we need to help change our student's perspective about how they use their time as well. #YOLO should bring new meaning to the phrase, "Use your time wisely."

## Prayer

*Heavenly Father, ignite a flame of passion within my heart to motivate my students. Help me bring them to the realization that time is an opportunity to get them closer to their God-given potential. Amen.*

# Day 24: Messenger of Hope

## Isaiah 43:18-19 (NLT)

*"But forget all that—it is nothing compared to what I am going to do. For I am about to do something new. See, I have already begun! Do you not see it? I will make a pathway through the wilderness. I will create rivers in the dry wasteland."*

When Isaiah the prophet relayed this message to the Children of Israel they were completely deflated and deficient of any hope about their future. The Northern Kingdom of Israel had been carried into captivity and the people were living in fear of impending destruction. However, in the middle of their desperation, Isaiah communicated a clear message of hope for their future. He encouraged them that God would give them a future so bright that it would overshadow the darkest moments of their current despair. Isaiah was the epitome of a messenger of hope.

As directors of destinies, educators are also obligated to become messengers of hope. There will come a point in time when a student enters your classroom dejected, defeated, and depressed. Under these conditions, learning will be almost impossible. So, how will you help the student manage his or her emotions while also focusing on the lesson at hand? Students may be young with a lot less responsibilities than adults but they still experience their own share of life stressors. Their feelings often overwhelm their judgment and obstruct their ability to think clearly (this also happens to adults). At these moments, teachers must allow their inner empathy and compassion to alter their instructional approach.

Sometimes a 2-minute deviation from the curriculum to provide a one-on-one message of hope is necessary to ensure that the particular student has an opportunity to learn the material being taught. Not to mention, this compassionate gesture can help to humanize teachers in the eyes of their students. This always makes providing future instruction a bit easier.

### Prayer

*Heavenly Father, I pray that you will use me today to be a messenger of hope. I do not know what my students have experienced throughout their life or throughout their day, but I ask for guidance as I show them that I care for them on a personal level. Amen.*

# Day 25: Finding Your Focus

## Proverbs 4:25 (NLT)

*"Look straight ahead, and fix your eyes on what lies before you."*

According to Julia Lawrence of Educationnews.org, students' development may be threatened by overstimulation caused by the "digital gadgetry" that has been integrated into every area of their lives.[xviii] Digital gadgetry would include the following: smartphones, smartwatches, smart boards, tablets, and many other forms of technology. Although these wonderful devices can help enhance the educational experience in schools, they may contribute to the overstimulation of students.

Overstimulation is typically applied to young children who are considered toddlers. It occurs when a child is inundated by more experiences, sensations, noises and activities that he or she can cope with.[xix] From a physical standpoint, overstimulation can cause children to feel tired or overwhelmed. From a neurological standpoint, overstimulation can cause the brain to produce a fear-based response in the amygdala.[xx] In addition, from a physiological standpoint, overstimulation impacts the central nervous system by heightening anxieties.

So, are most of the behavioral issues demonstrated by students linked to overstimulation? There is no research to prove this yet but the thought certainly has tremendous implications for neurologists, psychologists, and educators. Teachers in classrooms across the country, have noticed an increase in problematic behaviors that resemble anxiousness and attention deficits. In fact, The Center for Disease Control and Prevention notes, "The percentage of children with an Attention Deficit Hyperactivity Disorder (ADHD) diagnosis continues to increase from 7.8% in 2003 to 9.5% in 2007 and to 11% in 2011."[xxi]

Although there is no scientific proof to correlate the increase in ADHD diagnoses with the use of technological devices, it sheds light on the need to reduce distractions in order to help students find a central focus. Teachers can combat attention deficits by helping students improve their organizational skills, time management skills, and self-regulation skills. In addition, it would be prudent for teachers to set parameters for the use of technological devices in the classrooms.

**Prayer**

*Heavenly Father, grant me the patience, compassion, and perseverance to teach all of my students, especially those who exhibit attention deficits and behavioral problems. Teach me how to help them find their focus. Amen.*

# SECTION 5 REVIEW & APPLY

Explain which Bible verse from this section has helped you the most and why.

_____

_____

_____

_____

_____

Which prayer from this section has helped you the most and why?

_____

_____

_____

_____

_____

How will you apply what you have read this week?

_____

_____

_____

_____

_____

**Go to overcomingburnout.com and share your insight with the larger community!**

# SECTION 6 AFFIRMATION

## "I Will Overcome Burnout!"

### Isaiah 41:10 (NLT)

*"Don't be afraid, for I am with you. Don't be discouraged, for I am your God. I will strengthen you and help you. I will hold you up with my victorious right hand."*

## Practical Realization

When I played football in college, my strength and conditioning coach would encourage us to give our best effort in the weight room, especially when we felt physically exhausted. When we arrived at the end of our workouts (or at least when we thought we were finished), he would say, "Get on the floor in push-up position." Although it would seem as if every muscle in our bodies were twitching and shaking from exhaustion, we would have to position ourselves for more work. He would then say, "up" which would indicate holding our weight up in a push-up position. After we would complete a set of 10 he would shout, "Hold it, you still have more to give!" He would make us hold the very last push-up until we pushed ourselves to a point that we did not know existed.

It was in those moments of adversity that I learned the true meaning of "burn out." With sweat pouring off of my exhausted body, I realized that burnout means having absolutely nothing left in the tank. It is a feeling of utter weakness, where surrender is the only option left. I believe the same is true in the professional setting and I pray that you have not arrived at that point in your career. If you feel you are at a position of complete weakness, where surrendering is the only option, I encourage you, as my coach encouraged me: "Hold it! Because you still have more to give!" Push yourself to a point that you do not think exists. Latch on to God through the process and allow Him to give you the strength you need to make it through this rough patch. You will overcome burnout!

# Day 26: A Praying Teacher

## Psalm 120:1 (NLT)

*"I took my troubles to the LORD; I cried out to him, and he answered my prayer."*

Simply put, prayer is communicating with God. It is not a complex procedure that requires specific "church" jargon. You do not have to speak in Old English to communicate with God. All you have to do is speak to God similar to how you would speak to a very intimate friend. The only difference is this friend will never gossip about what you tell Him. He will never ignore your voice as if it is not valuable and worthy of attention. God will listen to you even when you take a long time to get to the main point (I do this all the time but God never rushes me).

In addition, God is unlike any friend in this world because He actually can help you no matter how big your problems may appear to be to you. God is all-powerful and there are no limits to what He can accomplish. Therefore, when you pray to God you can be assured that He can handle whatever has been troubling you. Whether it is job-related, family related, health-related, or all-the-above related, God can hear you and He can help you but you first must drive every issue into the presence of God through the vehicle of prayer. Prayer is the means by which an imperfect person can communicate with the perfect God of the universe.

Overcoming burnout will require a disciplined prayer life. How else will you maintain your joy, peace, and purpose as a teacher in the school systems of today? If anyone on the planet needs God, it's an educator! In fact, if you even begin to think about what you have to do at work this week you will automatically be one step closer to burnout. Unless, of course, you are fully relying on God to empower you to fulfill your purpose. This will require you to be in constant communication with God throughout each day. He will supply all of your needs and give you the peace you need to overcome burnout.

## Prayer

*Heavenly Father, teach me to pray daily for myself, my family, my students, and my coworkers. Remind me to bring all of my concerns to you with the understanding that you can exchange my problems for your peace. Amen.*

# Day 27: Peace on the Job

**Isaiah 26:3 (NLT)**

*"You will keep in perfect peace all who trust in you, all whose thoughts are fixed on you!"*

Peace is one of the most precious and prized possessions that a person can obtain. People yearn for peace on their jobs, in their homes, and in their relationships. It is definitely a vital human need. It is the state of tranquility, harmony, and freedom that is necessary to maintain quality mental health. It is the opposite of stress, frustration, and anxiety. Peace is necessary!

However, for many educators, peace is often elusive. Many educators struggle to maintain peace for 10 consecutive minutes at work because of a variety of factors. One of which is the presence of 20 to 30 energetic and talkative students. Other factors include: pressures from standardized testing criteria, financial stress, student loan debt, and life outside of school (marriage, parenting, health, etc.). For educators, the struggle is real!

Therefore, peace is one of the most valuable possessions any teacher can lay hold on. With seemingly a billion things left undone on your to-do-list, peace often appears buried under a host of issues. The fact that it is hidden implies that teachers must find time to dig and search for it if they desire to lay hold of it. This is where the problem lies. Where will you find the energy and time to dig for the peace that is hidden under a host of issues?

This is exactly why teachers need a personal and intimate relationship with God. God is the true source of peace. He freely gives peace to all who will trust in Him, all who fix their thoughts on God can have peace. God desires to consume you with the type of peace that surpasses all understanding but you have to focus your thoughts on God.

**Prayer**

*Heavenly Father, I ask that you supply me with your peace today. Give me peace on my job, in my home, and in my relationships. Help me to eliminate stress by relying on your strength. Amen.*

# Day 28: Handling Challenging Behavior

**2 Samuel 16:12 (NLT)**

*"And perhaps the Lord will see that I am being wronged
and will bless me because of these curses today."*

In the Old Testament, there was a man named Shimei who
was obviously having a bad day. Then he heard that King
David, who he had an issue with, was walking in the
vicinity of his village. Shimei came out cursing at David
and calling him all kinds of names because Shimei wanted
to blame David for something David was not even
responsible for: the death of one of his family members.
Although David had every reason to engage in a
confrontation with Shimei, he didn't. He simply said, "And
perhaps the Lord will see that I am being wronged and will
bless me because of these curses today."

David could not have handled the situation any
better. He chose to ignore the tantrum and the disrespect,
rather than taking it personal or allowing it to embitter him.
As educators we will be confronted with challenging
behaviors on a weekly basis (some of us on a daily basis)
but how we respond to each challenge will ultimately shape
the perception that we hold of our job. How we feel about

our job will be dictated by our experiences on our job. Do you wake up feeling joyful about what the new workday will bring your way or do you wake up frustrated by the fact that the student who challenges you the most will be in class today?

If you connect more with the latter question, I encourage you to be like David. Ignore the behavior but do not tolerate it. There is never room for disrespect in your classroom but do not take the challenging behavior personally. Seek to understand it. Always remember, all behavior is communication. Sometimes challenging behaviors from students are merely misdirected frustrations stemming from a variety of internal issues. It could be fueled by family issues, self-esteem issues, or issues related to trying to fit in with peer groups. I am not saying you should volunteer to be a student's punching bag by any means, but I am saying you should be focused on looking beyond the punches to understand their intent.

Students, like adults, carry their own pain from past experiences and "hurt people tend to hurt people" (or at least try to hurt people). This applies to your students as well as your co-workers but consider this: Maybe God will bless you for how you have been treated.

# Prayer

*Heavenly Father, help me maintain my integrity and lead me to take the high road during conflicts on my job. Protect my heart from bitterness and resentment whenever I encounter challenging behaviors, whether with my students, their parents, or my co-workers. Help me to understand that not all attacks are personal. Amen.*

# Day 29: Thank God for Extra Help!

**Psalm 16:8 (NLT)**

*"I know the Lord is always with me. I will not be shaken,
for he is right beside me."*

The Christian concept of the Trinity can seem very
perplexing to most people, especially math teachers. This
is because the Trinity introduces a math equation that
means $3 = 1$. It applies to the fact that Christians affirm
that God is one and yet He manifests as three distinct
persons: God, the Father, God, the Son, and God, the Holy
Spirit. Although the Father, the Son, and the Holy Spirit
are equal in authority, they serve different functions or
roles.

The Holy Spirit is the very presence of God in the
earth realm. He is present and active in the lives of all
Christians. He is personally responsible for leading us into
all truth. Yet, the Holy Spirit is not a physical being, nor is
He bound to the natural laws concerning matter. He is
Spirit and therefore functions in a spiritual dimension
outside of the boundaries of earth. However, He is able to
influence the natural world in profound ways. This means
that although the Holy Spirit is not tangible, His influence

and activities are real and experiential in the lives of all believers.

The Holy Spirit has come to the earth to serve as a helper, which means every Christian has access to the extra help that is necessary to fulfill purpose on earth. God knows teachers need extra help to manage their families and their classrooms! No person can be effective in every area of life without a little extra help. So, thank God for the Holy Spirit who desires to be our supernatural helper.

**Prayer**

*Heavenly Father, I thank you for sending the Holy Spirit into my life. I pray that you will help me to rely on Him to lead, guide, and strengthen me as I seek to fulfill my purpose. Amen.*

# Day 30: Standardized Anxieties

**Philippians 4:6 (NASB)**

*"Be anxious for nothing, but in everything by prayer and supplication with thanksgiving let your requests be made known to God. And the peace of God, which surpasses all comprehension, will guard you hearts and your minds in Christ Jesus."*

For most people, overcoming burnout will depend heavily on their ability to manage their own anxieties. According to The American Heritage Dictionary of the English Language, anxiety is "A state of uneasiness and apprehension, as about future uncertainties."[xxii] Simply put, anxieties are worries. As soon as we begin to worry or express concern, we are already anxious and if we are anxious, we are one step closer to experiencing burnout.

Burnout is considered to be the main cause for the mass exodus of many qualified and competent teachers. The good news is not all teachers who feel burnt out leave the field altogether. The bad news is some choose to hang around and constantly identify new things to complain about. Obviously, this is just as bad as leaving and sometimes worst because of the detrimental impact these teachers can have on other teachers, as well as students.

So, what causes burnout? There is no easy answer to this question, but one thing is true. When teachers are polled about what causes burnout, many will mention standardized testing. In today's world, there is an enormous amount of pressure placed on teachers to get their students to pass rigorous state-sanctioned standardized tests. In some cases, these tests are used to assess the overall performance of teachers. This means that a teacher can lose his or her job if his or her students perform poorly on a test.

The pressures of standardized testing are an enormous source of tension and stress in the lives of educators. From teachers, to administrators, to the highest ranking school officials, everyone is feeling the pressures of standardized testing. These intense pressures can create a hostile and unpleasant work environment for educators. With these types of pressures placed on educators, it is easy to see why teachers become frustrated and overwhelmed with anxieties. This is one of the reasons why all teachers must be praying teachers.

## Prayer

*Heavenly Father, I pray that you will shower me with the peace that defies comprehension. Help me to overcome the anxieties and pressures placed upon me as an educator. Amen.*

# SECTION 6 REVIEW & APPLY

Explain which Bible verse from this section has helped you
the most and why.

_____
_____
_____
_____
_____

Which prayer from this section has helped you the most
and why?

_____
_____
_____
_____
_____

How will you apply what you have read this week?

_____
_____
_____
_____
_____

**Go to overcomingburnout.com and share your insight with the
larger community!**

# REAL-LIFE STUDENT STORIES

**Larry, an 18-year-old high school student, stated:**

*"Dear Mrs. Johnson,*
*I am so glad to have you as my teacher. You have helped*
*me understand that I can be anything I want to be in life as*
*long as I try. When I first came to your class I was scared*
*and nervous because I had never played an instrument in*
*my life. But you have helped me realize that it is not that*
*hard. Thank you.*

**Sarah, a 13-year-old eighth-grade student, stated:**

*"Mr. Martinez,*
*I don't know if you realize it or not but you have changed*
*the way I see school. Before I took your class I hated*
*school and I hated math. No matter how hard I tried, it*
*was always a weakness for me. But you showed me that I*
*can do it. I never told you before but thanks for*
*everything."*

**Chelsea, a 14-year-old sophomore in high school, stated:**

*"Hey Mrs. Sanders,*
*You are awesome! You have taught me so much over the*
*last 9 weeks. I have even learned the difference between a*

*plant cell and an animal cell, which is crazy! I have also learned a lot about myself. I will never forget the day when you gave me a hug and told me everything was going to be alright. After my parents divorced I was struggling to hold myself together but your words of encouragement helped me a lot. I truly appreciate you!"*

**Terrell, 15-year-old ninth grader, stated:**

*"Hello Mrs. White,*
*I just want to thank you for being my teacher this year. I still don't like English but at least you were a cool teacher. You were always there for me even after I was moved from your class. Thanks for the support and I look forward to seeing you next year. Enjoy your summer!*

# CONCLUSION

It is not uncommon to feel unappreciated or underappreciated on your job. As teachers, you may rarely hear your students thank you for what you do. This is not to say that your students are not thankful to have you as their teacher. It's just that many of your students will not recognize the impact you are making in their lives until they leave your class. Sometimes, students never acknowledge how they feel about you but that does not mean they do not think about it themselves. For example, how many teachers have you had in your life that you actually thanked for inspiring you? Not many. Yet, you appreciate everything they did for you despite the fact that you never told them. The same is true for your students.

As you strive to overcome burnout, I pray that this book, will be one resource to help you find strength as you seek to reach and teach all of your students. I encourage you to incorporate all of the Bible verses, prayers, and practical insights found on these pages into your daily life. In addition, write the affirmations found in each section somewhere in your journal, on your workroom desk, or in your classroom. These positive and powerful affirmations will help you maintain the proper perspective of your job, especially when burnout tries to creep into your mind.

1. I AM A TEACHER WITH A PURPOSE
2. I AM A COORDINATOR OF COMPASSION
3. I AM A FACILITATOR OF LEARNING
4. I AM A CULTIVATOR OF CHARACTER
5. I AM A DIRECTOR OF DESTINIES
6. I WILL OVERCOME BURNOUT!

**Philippians 4:8-9 (NIV)**

*"Finally, brothers and sisters, whatever is true, whatever is noble, whatever is right, whatever is pure, whatever is lovely, whatever is admirable—if anything is excellent or praiseworthy—think about such things. Whatever you have learned or received or heard from me, or seen in me—put into practice. And the God of peace will be with you."*

# MEET THE AUTHOR

Jahkari "JT" Taylor has worked in the field of education since he was 19 years old. He began his career as a paraprofessional/teacher assistant working with students who have been identified with emotional/behavioral disabilities while he completed his undergraduate degree at Norfolk State University. As soon as he graduated and obtained his teaching license he was working full-time as a special education teacher.

JT is now the CEO of Purpose Pushers LLC, which is a hybrid educational consulting company that couples research-based professional development with motivational speaking. JT was the 2017 City-Wide Teacher of the Year for Chesapeake Public Schools and is an emerging leader in the field of education. He is a highly sought-after speaker who has presented at numerous schools, universities, and professional conferences across the state of Virginia. He has been featured in a WHRO commercial titled, "The Teaching Profession" and JT has also published numerous books including: *Overcoming Burnout, True Leaders LEAD, Becoming One Flesh, Relational Teaching, and 7 Traits of a Teacher with a Purpose.* JT has committed his life to motivating and inspiring people from all walks of life by helping them discover their unique purpose. His motto is simple, "Know Your Why."

For speaking engagements, keynotes, or professional developments, JT can be reached at jtwithapurpose@gmail.com or at www.purposepushers.com.

# BIBLIOGRAPHY/SOURCES

[i] Maurice J. Elias, "Teacher burnout: what are the warning signs." Edutopia, May 23, 2012. Accessed May 1, 2016, http://www.edutopia.org/blog/teacher-burnout-warning-signs-maurice-elias

[ii] Biblehub. "3339. Metamorphoo." Accessed May 1, 2016, http://biblehub.com/greek/3339.htm

[iii] Biblehub. "342 anakainósis." Accessed May 1, 2016, http://biblehub.com/greek/342.htm

[iv] Biblehub "3101. Mathetes." Accessed May 1, 2016, http://biblehub.com/greek/3101.htm

[v] Ibid., 93

[vi] http://www.bullyingstatistics.org/content/bullying-and-suicide.html

[vii] Ibid.

[viii] Ibid.

[ix] http://caroltomlinson.com/

[x] Institute of Public Health in Ireland. "Health impacts of education: A review." November 2008 accessed on May 3, 2016 from http://www.publichealth.ie/publications/healthimpactsofeducationareview

[xi] Ungemah, Lori, "What is Academic Rigor?!," *Huffington Post -The Blog* July 19, 2012. Accessed on May 9, 2016 from http://www.huffingtonpost.com/lori-ungemah/what-is-academic-rigor_b_1686412.html

[xii] http://www.brainyquote.com/quotes/quotes/m/martinluth402936.html

[xiii] "Self-Discipline." Accessed on 05/10/2016 from https://ahdictionary.com/word/search.html?q=self+discipline

[xiv] Duckworth, Angela L., and Martin EP Seligman. "Self-discipline outdoes IQ in predicting academic performance of adolescents." *Psychological science* 16, no. 12 (2005): 939-944. Accessed from http://pss.sagepub.com/content/16/12/939.short

[xv] Duckworth, Angela Lee. "The Key to Success? Grit." *Ted Talks Education*, April 2013. Accessed May 11, 2016 from https://www.ted.com/talks/angela_lee_duckworth_the_key_to_success_grit?language=en

[xvi] Ibid.

[xvii] http://genhq.com/FAQ-info-about-generations/

[xviii] Lawrence, Julia "Technology could lead to overstimulation in kids." *Education News*. June 2012. Accessed May 12, 2016 from www.educationnews.org/parenting/technology-could-lead-to-overstimulation-in-kids/

[xix] "Overstimulation: babies and children." RaisingChildren.net.au. Accessed from on May 12, 2016 from http://m.raisingchilden.net.au/articles/overstimulation.html.

[xx] "Is social anxiety caused by overstimulation?" *Mental Health Daily* (no date) Accessed on May 12, 2016 from http://mentalhealthdaily.com/2014/03/21/is-social--anxiety-caused-by-overstimulation/

[xxi] Center for Disease Control and Prevention. "Data and Statistics." Accessed from www.cdc.gov/ncbddd/adhd/data.html

[xxii] "Anxieties." *The American Heritage Dictionary of the English Language*. Accessed on May 12, 2016 from https://ahdictionary.com/word/search.html?q=anxiety